CHR
PATF

CHRIS TEMPLE, PATROL LEADER

by

IVY F. E. MIDDLETON

VICTORY PRESS
LONDON AND EASTBOURNE

Revised edition 1969

SBN 85476 056 3

Printed in Great Britain for
VICTORY PRESS (Evangelical Publishers Ltd.)
Lottbridge Drove, Eastbourne,
by Compton Printing Ltd.,
London and Aylesbury

CONTENTS

CHAPTER I

A HURRIED MEAL

CHRIS lifted a crimson face from her hanky.

"Sorry, Mums," she said contritely. "A crumb went down the wrong way."

Her mother raised her eyebrows.

"It's not like you to bolt your food, dear," she said mildly. "You've been rushing ever since I said Grace. Colin's not home from school yet. You've plenty of time, haven't you?"

"Not really, Mummy," Chris told her. "We're starting Guides earlier this evening because we're doing outdoor tests for part of the meeting. But I didn't realize I was rushing so! Oh, here's Colin now."

They both looked towards the door as heavy footsteps sounded outside. Almost immediately it opened and Chris's brother strode in. His mop of copper-coloured hair, which earned him the name of Coppernob at school, was in direct contrast to Chris's smooth, dark hair, but they both had the same merry brown eyes.

"I say!" he greeted his mother and sister in an indignant voice. "What do you think? I've had my bike confiscated at school. The police came and carried out an inspection of all the cycles while we were at Assembly, and mine went to join six other 'old crocks' outside the Head's study. The report said that no repairs could rectify them and we were on no account to use them again."

Chris chuckled unsympathetically.

"It's just as well, I should think. You were a menace to the public, riding that thing! I can't think why you didn't get rid of it long ago," she added candidly.

Colin grinned good-naturedly and dropped into a chair at the table. "Because no one would have it! I once considered inserting an advertisement in the local paper: Cycle for sale. Five shillings, or would exchange for a reliable camel."

As their sudden peal of laughter died away, he added, "You needn't be so superior, anyway, young Chris, just because you've got your Cyclist badge. Isn't this your Guide night, by the way?"

"Yes!" Chris drained her cup and glanced at her watch. "We've got a Sealed Orders evening, working in pairs. I expect I'll be partnering Bunny, as she's our littlest Guide. I usually do."

"Why 'Bunny'?" Colin wanted to know. "Is she a direct descendant of John Bunyan, or something?"

ing and hiking, bigger than good turns and gaining badges—bigger even than winning the coveted Patrol prize. Was it the ideals that lay behind it, that made it so special? she wondered. The ideals —and the sense of adventure?

Still pursuing this train of thought, she stepped into her navy-blue skirt. Then she adjusted her scarlet triangular scarf and pinned her Promise badge on to it. No-one could say the Guide uniform was not 'with it', she reflected.

Slowly she said the Guide Promise to herself, savouring each clause: "I promise that I will do my best, to do my duty to God, to serve the Queen and help other people, and to keep the Guide Law."

Then she went on to the Guide Law: loyalty, helpfulness, consideration, friendliness, kindness to animals and respect to all living things, obedience, courage and cheerfulness in all difficulties, making good use of one's time, taking care of one's own and other people's possessions—and finally self-control.

Could one really live up to that standard—always? she wondered, a little wistfully. She did so want to be an out-and-out Guide. Like the World Chief Guide, with her glowing personality and infectious enthusiasm. It had been Chris's ambition when she was only a Tenderfoot. Now that she was a Patrol Leader it was heaps more important.

Perhaps there was some secret she might stumble upon one day, if she were sufficiently alert? Her face brightened at the thought. Then, giving a rub to her already shiny brown shoes, she hurried downstairs.

CHAPTER 2

FIVE SEALED ENVELOPES

CHRIS instinctively checked her wrist watch as the church clock chimed the hour.

"We're not doing badly for time," she told her small partner, "thanks to your powers of observation! I shouldn't have had a clue about the famous artist if it hadn't been for you."

On leaving the Guide Hut the two Poppies had made their way directly to the cottage bearing a plaque stating that a well-known artist had once lived there, and they had recorded his name and dates in their note-books, as directed by the slip of paper in the first sealed envelope. It so happened that Bunny had noticed the plaque when visiting an aunt in that area only a week or two earlier, and so the pair had been able to save several valuable minutes.

Bunny beamed at the praise.

"But I wasn't v-very good at filling in the street names on that b-blank map, for the second test," she reminded her Leader. "What do we have to do n-next?"

Chris quickly slit the third sealed envelope and

ready aloud from the paper inside: "*Proceed to a well-known building with a weather-vane. Fifty-five yards to the north-east of the corner on which the building stands you will find a stranger needing assistance. Give her the help she requires. She will then hand you two sealed envelopes.*"

"A weather-vane," murmured Chris.

"There's one on the B-bowls Pavilion," Bunny said eagerly. "I saw it last Saturday. It's in the shape of a m-man stooping to bowl."

Chris shook her head. "That won't do. It's not on a corner. The Public Library's more like it, and I don't think it's got a weather-vane. I wonder which other building has one?"

She looked up at the church clock for inspiration, as she spoke. Then she started and a broad smile spread over her face. Above their heads a weather-vane moved gently in the wind!

Quickly the Poppies paced out the required distance and found themselves standing outside a chemist's shop.

"Good evening," Lieutenant greeted them, stepping from the doorway. "Can you direct me to the nearest call-box, please?"

Bunny stared at her in astonishment.

"But you know w-where it is!" she exclaimed. Then she realized that Lieutenant was the 'stranger' whom they were to help, and she hastily changed her tune. "Oh, yes, c-certainly. It's in the High Street. On a corner, about three or f-four turnings up."

Lieutenant looked at her quizzically. "I'm a stranger here. Remember? *You* have a go, Chris, and see if you can be more explicit."

Chris was ready for the challenge. She had been rehearsing the directions while Bunny was making her attempt.

"Take the first turning on the right, and the second on the left," she said briskly. "That brings you to the High Street. You'll find the phone box on the third street corner on the left, You can't miss it. The turning's called James Street."

"Splendid!" the Guider commented. She held out two sealed envelopes. "Here are your fourth and fifth tests. Don't open them until you get to the top of this road. Off you go, both of you."

The pair lost no time in obeying her injunction. At the end of the road Chris hastily slit the envelope marked No. 4. The half sheet of notepaper inside was typed, and it read: *Go to the place where willow and leather meet. Write the name of that place in your note-books. Then sit on the nearest seat and memorize the message printed below. Deliver it verbally to Mrs. Harman, at 5, The Avenue.*

"That's Captain's mother," she informed

Bunny. "But where's the place where willows and leather meet?"

Bunny looked at her blankly. Suddenly they both spoke together.

"The Recreation Ground."

"The p-pond."

"It *must* be the p-pond, Chris," Bunny pointed out excitedly. "That's where the willow trees are. There's a s-seat near it, too."

"Not so fast, little one," Chris restrained her. "You're a good soul to remember the trees, but it might be a false scent. There's no leather there—unless it's leather shoes climbing up the trees," she added with a grin. "There's always some little urchin or other tree-climbing in this neighbourhood!"

Suddenly she caught Bunny's arm. "It *is* the Recreation Ground. Cricket bats are made of willow and cricket balls of leather; and that's where cricket matches are held. Quick—run!"

Five minutes later they dropped panting into a seat. They wrote 'Recreation Ground' in their note-books and then poured over the printed message. It was brief and to the point: *Dial 999. Ask for Police and tell them there has been an accident at the crossroads, by the Children's Home. Two cars and a motor-scooter are involved, and an ambulance will be needed.*

Chris slowly read it aloud three times, while Bunny repeated it phrase by phrase. Then, having both got it by heart, they hurried to 5, The Avenue. Mrs. Harman opened the door, a broad smile on her face.

"We've a message for you," said Chris quickly.

She repeated it word for word and waited to see what would happen next.

"I'd like your partner to give it to me, too," Mrs. Harman requested. "Just to confirm the details, you know."

Bunny was ready, and she rattled off the message at a fine speed.

A twinkle peeped out of Mrs. Harman's eyes for a moment. Then she said, "Now give me your note-books and I'll enter your score. Nine points out of ten."

Bunny's face fell. She was so sure they had earned full marks. And Chris, exchanging a rueful little smile with Mrs. Harman, had not the heart to tell her smallest Patrol member that Bunny had lost the precious point herself by saying, "Dial 99".

As they left the house, Chris slit the final envelope and glanced quickly at the slip of paper inside. It read: *Make your way back to the Guide Hut, pausing en route to collect the signature of a woman or girl out walking with her dog. If you fail to see one, come back without the signature—but lose a point!*"

"Not if I know it!" said Chris. "There's simply got to be a woman with a dog somewhere on the last lap. Come on. Let's start back."

They walked briskly, keeping their eyes open. A small boy came racing past with a puppy on a string, and two mongrels rushed out of a side turning, in playful mood. But of a woman and dog there was no sign.

Suddenly Bunny clutched her arm.

"Th-there's one!" she almost shouted.

A young woman had suddenly turned the corner and was coming towards them at a smart pace, her head thrown back.

Then their faces fell. The dog, a yellow Labrador, was wearing a white harness and obviously leading its mistress.

"It's a Guide Dog," said Chris, the hope fading from her eyes. "She must be blind."

"And she w-won't be able to write," added Bunny tragically.

Chris made a sudden decision.

"Some blind people can sign their names," she said. "We'll have to chance it, anyway. It's our only hope!"

CHAPTER 3

PATROL PLANS

"WASN'T she l-lovely!" exclaimed Bunny with enthusiasm, a few minutes later, as the pair hurried towards the Guide Hut. "When you spoke to her she s-sort of lighted up all over."

Chris nodded vigorously.

"I wouldn't have known she was blind if it hadn't been for the dog's white harness—she had such beautiful eyes," she returned. "I wish we could have stopped to chat with her. Wasn't it good that she could sign her name? It's perfectly readable, even if it's a bit crooked. *Andrea Whitfield.* That'll get us a point all right."

As she spoke, they turned into the Guide Hut and joined a bevy of Guides who were clustered around Captain.

"Ah! Chris and Bunny," said the Guider, holding out her hand for their note-books and street map. "I can't work out the final points till Lieutenant comes in with her report, but you shall all have the results before we dismiss. Did you enjoy yourselves?"

"Rather!" they told her cheerfully.

The other Poppies arrived back shortly afterwards, and for the next few minutes there was an excited buzz of conversation in their Patrol Corner as the three pairs compared notes. Elizabeth's face fell as they discussed the fourth test. She and Julie had made straight for the pond!

"It looks as if we haven't done too badly, all the same," said Sandra, Chris's Patrol Second, her round, good-tempered face beaming happily. "I hope Lieutenant gets back soon. The rest of the Pansies and Fuchsias are in now."

Their conclave was interrupted by Captain's whistle signal, "Leaders come here!" and Chris ran forward, eager to know what was to happen next. Five minutes later she was back in the Poppies' Corner, her face flushed with excitement.

"We've got to go into a huddle on the subject of Patrol Service," she announced, "and think up something very special we can do to help others during the coming months. I'm all for it! We haven't done much in the way of a Patrol Good Deed since we bought those new-laid eggs at Easter and took them round to sick folk. Let's plan something really special."

There was a little silence during which they all looked hopefully at one another. Then Sandra rubbed her snub nose reflectively and said, "I could suggest something, but you might not think it a good idea."

"Let's hear it," commanded Chris.

Her Second needed no further invitation.

"Daddy's got friendly lately with the new owner of *The Hollies*, the big house near the crossroads," she told them. "His name's Sir Roderick, and he's very keen on helping blind people. He's specially interested in The Guide Dogs for the Blind Association and he gave Daddy a lot of literature about it."

Bunny opened her mouth to speak of Miss Whitfield and her Guide Dog, but she closed it again as she realized that Sandra had news to impart.

The Second continued: "One of the leaflets said that sometimes Scouts and Guides make collections of silver paper, milk-bottle tops, and pie cases, and sell them to raise money to train Guide Dogs and their owners. I was going to tell Captain about it, but I won't if you think we could do it for our Patrol Service."

The Poppies exchanged glances.

"I like the idea!" said Chris. "I was thinking only the other day that I'd like to work for the Friend to the Blind badge if I can manage to learn braille. Nearly every time there's a lovely sunset I think how dreadful it must be not to be able to see it!"

"And not to be able to see friendly smiles, either," put in Sandra. "Blind people are usually wonderfully cheerful, though. I've just been reading about Fanny Crosby, the hymn-writer. She went blind when she was only six, and when she was eight she wrote her first poem:

Oh, what a happy soul I am;
Although I cannot see,
I am resolved that in this world
Contented I will be.

It made me think, I can tell you!"

There was a sympathetic little silence. Then Julie said slowly, "I think it would be grand to help a blind person, but wouldn't it take an awful lot of milk-bottle tops and things to get enough money for a Guide Dog? Tin-foil is awfully light, and I expect the milk-bottle tops and things would be sold by weight."

"But we've got the whole district to collect from," her sister Shirley pointed out. "We could each have our own evening for collecting. That would be six evenings a week, and we could buy a street map and plan a proper campaign. We've got bikes, and lots of people would save their tin-foil and let us call for it regularly. Can you remember anything else it said in the leaflet, Sandra?"

The Patrol Second fumbled in her pocket.

"I brought the leaflet down to show Captain," she told her. "If we take it on we can name one of the Association's puppies. And when it's a properly trained Guide Dog and we've reached our money target, they'll send us a framed photograph of the dog."

Chris beamed happily. "We'll hang it in our Patrol Corner. How much money do we have to collect, Sandra?"

The Second hesitated.

"Rather a lot, I'm afraid," she admitted. "It costs about £250 to provide a trained Guide Dog—and to train the blind person and dog together. As we collect the tin-foil, we send it in sacks direct to the smelters. Then they tell The Guide Dogs for the Blind Association how much money to credit us with."

"Two hundred and fifty *pounds*?" gasped Julie. "We'd all be in the Senior Branch before we could raise that amount!"

"That's defeatism," remarked Elizabeth severely. "If other Guides and Scouts have tackled it, so can we!"

"And we could do other th-things to raise

money at the same time," Bunny pointed out excitedly. "Oh, do let's t-take it on. Chris and I saw a Guide Dog leading a blind w-woman this evening, and it was lovely!"

Her green eyes were glowing like lanterns in her pointed little face.

"I think it's a challenge to the Poppies," said Chris, decidedly. "If we really care about blind people we'll attempt it, however impossible it seems!"

"Well, *I'm* willing," said Elizabeth.

Chris beamed. "Good girl! What about the rest of you? Those in favour say aye."

"Aye!" came a chorus from the others.

"That's settled, then." The P.L. thought rapidly. "Come round to my home at 6 o'clock tomorrow and we'll have a Patrol meeting to plan the campaign. Bunny had better not go collecting alone; she's too young. We'll each take it in turns to have her with us. I think——"

A series of staccato blasts from Captain's whistle cut her short, and the Guides raced to the centre of the hut, where the Guider stood waiting to announce the results of the Sealed Orders Tests.

She smiled as she saw their eager faces. "I won't keep you in suspense. The Poppies came first—by a single point! The Fuchsias were second, and the Pansies came just two points below them. Well done, Poppies!"

"It was Miss Whitfield's signature got us that deciding point," Chris whispered to Bunny under cover of the buzz of conversation which followed the announcement. "I guess it's a sign that we're right to take on that Guide Dog challenge. We'll see it through, even if we burst in the attempt!"

CHAPTER 4

THANKS TO BUNNY

"YOUR devotion to duty astounds me," Colin announced with a comical lift of an eyebrow, a couple of evenings later. "What are you all dressed up for this time? Not another Company meeting, surely?"

Chris picked up a bulging haversack. "No—a Patrol one. I'm taking the Poppies up to Mr. Blake's meadow to practise fire-lighting for Second Class. He said we could."

Colin looked impressed. "There's no holding the Poppets, now that they've got a new leader. I hope you've studied your subject thoroughly. Remember, a small punk tin filled with dried birch bark, dead holly leaves, and gorse twigs will ensure that the fire burns whatever the weather. Syrup tins are easily converted into billies, and—— *Ow!*"

Chris had flung herself at him and was tugging at his mop of flaming hair.

"You've been reading my copy of *The Guide*," she accused him. "I've been hunting everywhere for it!"

Colin grinned. "Well, if you *will* leave your *Bunty's Own* around where your big brother can lay hands on it, you must expect him to take advantage of a little self-education. Here, take it, my child, and go. It's ten to seven. I presume you're meeting the other Poppets at seven?"

"Poppies," Chris patiently corrected him. "Yes. See you later. 'Bye!"

Five minutes Scout's pace—alternate running and walking—brought her to the meadow just as the others began to arrive. She and Sandra had gathered the wood on the previous evening, and had broken it into short lengths. Now, under a groundsheet, it was lying neatly across two long, thick sticks, to keep it off the damp ground.

"We've graded the wood," Chris pointed out to Julie and Shirley, "from thin pieces at one end to thick pieces at the other, so you'll have no excuse for letting the fire go out. Here's Sandra now with the punk tin, and Bunny just behind her. Sandra, will you cut out a good-sized area of turf? About eighteen inches square should be ample. We'll start with a pyramid fire and then we'll convert it into a cobhouse. Bunny, you can light the punk when we've laid it. Not more than two matches, mind!"

Bunny's first attempt at fire-lighting failed, for she had omitted to shield the flame from the light wind. At her second attempt, however, the dry punk blazed up.

"I wish we'd brought some food to cook," said Elizabeth, arriving on the scene as the punk set light to the kindling and then to the sticks. "We could have cooked it in the ashes when the fire died down."

Chris raised a heated face from the proximity of the flames.

"We shan't have time this evening, but we'll have a Patrol hike one Saturday soon," she promised her. "Then we'll cook dampers, and toasted cheese dreams, and heaps of other things."

"Siskabobs, too," said Sandra enthusiastically.

"And p-poached eggs in half orange skins," added Bunny, not to be outdone, "and s-sausages cooked on green sticks!"

Chris looked at her watch. "We will, but the next thing on the programme for *you*, my infant, is to follow a trail I laid for you earlier this evening, beginning just the other side of that hedge. I want to see if you really know the tracking signs."

Bunny's green eyes glowed with excitement.

"W-will you time me?" she asked.

Without waiting for a reply, she set off eagerly in the direction indicated, and Chris turned her attention to the other Poppies.

As soon as the fire was going really well, she left Sandra to keep an eye on it while she demonstrated to the others how to lay an Indian fire, a crane fire, a lazyman fire, and an A fire. Then Sandra took over and showed them how to make a toaster from a green stick, and a grill for cooking meat over a wood fire.

Meanwhile, Bunny was eagerly following Chris's trail. The P.L. had used materials from the fields and hedgerows to make her signs, and the youngest Poppy had to keep her eyes wide open to spot such indications as a leaf with a twig through it, a small arrow made from twigs, a group of stones, and marks scratched here and there, in muddy places, with a stick.

"Follow this path as far as it goes," Bunny murmured to herself, and then quickly dispersed the stones that had given her the message. She chuckled gleefully to herself. Chris was going to be pleased with her, she decided.

"Message hidden five paces this way," she muttered, a few minutes later, her eyes searching the ground. And pacing it out, she discovered a stone half-buried in the earth, close to a public footpath. Beneath it she found a piece of folded paper, but, as she stooped to pick it up, her keen eyes spotted something reflecting the light of the evening sun.

Ignoring the paper, Bunny reached for the little object, and her eyes became as round as saucers.

"My!" she breathed.

Quickly she slipped it into her pocket and buttoned it down firmly. Then, all thought of the trail forgotten, she turned about and ran swiftly back to where the Poppies were finishing their lesson in fire-laying.

Chris looked at her in amazement as she arrived, panting.

"You've been very quick," she said suspiciously. "Did you follow the trail right to where I left the I-have-gone-home sign?"

"No, I f-found something and I came b-back," Bunny burst out, her face crimson from running. "It was close by the f-footpath. Look!"

The Poppies crowded round as she dived into her pocket and pulled out her find.

"Whew!" whistled Chris.

"An emerald brooch!" breathed Julie.

The P.L. held out her hand for it.

"It wouldn't be a *real* one, silly!" she laughed. "Probably bought from a chain store. But it's rather attractive, isn't it! We'd better take it to the police station. I expect the owner will be pleased to have it back."

"But we can't go away and leave the fire like this," objected Sandra. "It wouldn't be safe."

"You certainly can't," agreed Chris promptly. "Not until the ash is cold, anyway. And you'd better water it, too, before you put back the turf. There's a bottle of water in my haversack. It doesn't need six of us to take one small brooch to the police station. Bunny must go, because she found it; and I'll go with her."

Seeing their disappointed faces, she added, "Don't look so down in the mouth. You won't be missing much. All the policeman will do is to take the brooch from us and write down a few particulars in a book."

Ten minutes' sharp walk brought the two Poppies to the police station. As Chris anticipated, the officer on duty opened a large book.

"You do the t-talking," Bunny whispered to her.

The policeman inspected the brooch closely. Then he looked keenly at the two eager faces before him.

"And you say you found it this evening, just off the public footpath running through Mr. Blake's land," he said. "You must have very good eyesight if it was hidden in the long grass!"

"My friend was tracking," Chris explained. "It just happened that I'd left a woodcraft sign close by, so she was searching there."

The police officer nodded, evidently satisfied, and made an entry in the book.

"The brooch was lost over a week ago," he told them. "Have you any idea of its value?"

Chris hesitated. "Not really. Fairly cheap, I thought. Five shillings?"

A broad smile illuminated his homely features. "My wife would like to buy one at that figure! It's a genuine emerald!"

Their mouths dropped open with surprise, and he added cheerfully, "What's more, young ladies, there is a £20 reward offered for its recovery. You'll be coming into money quite shortly!"

When they had recovered sufficiently from their astonishment to find their tongues, both Poppies spoke at once.

"B-but——"

"We can't take money for a good deed!"

It was the policeman's turn to look surprised.

"That's the first time I've ever known anyone to refuse money," he told them. "You'll have earned it, anyway; and I don't suppose there's anything in your rules against earning money, is there? What about the Scouts with their bob-a-job week?"

Observing that the Poppies still hesitated, he suggested helpfully, "Haven't you some charity you're interested in, if you don't feel you can put the reward into your pockets?"

Chris and Bunny exchanged sudden, excited glances, all their indecision gone. The same thought was in both their minds.

Here was the first contribution to their new Guide Dog Fund!

CHAPTER 5

THE CAMPAIGN BEGINS

"I THINK it's exciting!" said Bunny. "Even if we haven't got much t-tin-foil yet, ever so many people have promised to save their bottle tops and p-pie cases for us. And the greengrocer gave us a s-sack for nothing, instead of charging us sixpence or a sh-shilling!"

It was exactly two evenings since the Poppies had decided on their Patrol service, and Chris and Bunny were already on the job. With Captain's permission they had donned their Guide uniforms, suspecting that they would get a better reception and more support if they went in an official capacity.

"Not tired yet?" Chris asked her. "I'd planned another half hour, but I can finish alone if you'd like to call it a day?"

Bunny shook her head vigorously.

"I needn't be home for n-nearly an hour yet," she said stoutly, "and I'm n-not a bit tired. Where do we go next?"

Chris consulted the map. "Mayfield Road, and then on to the cottages at the bottom of the hill.

Here, let me take the sack. You're falling over it!"

The Mayfield Road residents proved, on the whole, to be satisfyingly responsive, and the two Poppies left the road with a number of promises in their note-books and a little tin-foil in the sack.

"Ooh, do l-let's go to that cottage over there," cried Bunny, as they reached the foot of the hill. "I'm sure somebody nice must l-live there. It's a real picture p-postcard place!"

Chris readily agreed, and a few moments later they were knocking on the door. It was opened almost immediately by a smiling, young woman with a yellow Labrador at her side.

"Miss Whitfield!" exclaimed the Poppies in surprise.

"Is it the Guides?" Andrea asked, a note of pleasure in her soft, musical voice. "I thought I recognized your voices! Do come in."

She led them into a cosy sitting-room and settled them in deep armchairs. Then she sat on the sofa, with her dog, Judy, lying at her feet.

"We called because we're doing a house-to-house collection of tin-foil," Chris said, a little shyly, after she'd explained that they hadn't known she lived there. "It's to help to provide blind people with Guide Dogs, and to train the dogs and their owners."

Andrea Whitfield's sensitive face lighted up.

"That's splendid!" she said. "Do go on. I'm most interested."

In a few words the P.L. outlined their Patrol campaign.

"You say it is your Patrol Service," Miss Whitfield said thoughtfully. "Is it competitive—to gain points for your Patrol?"

"Oh, no!" came the quick reply from both Poppies, and Chris added, "It's to encourage the Company to help other people. To foster a spirit of service, Captain said."

"And you'd be allowed to have help?" Andrea waited for their assent and continued, "Then I can put you on to someone who will be a real help to you. More important still, you'll be of tremendous assistance to *him*! I mean Sir Roderick, at *The Hollies*. His sister, Miss Carson, used to be District Commissioner for the Northoaks Guides before her illness. I lived quite near them for some years and we became very friendly. I moved out here last Christmas, and I was awfully pleased when they followed in the spring!"

The Poppies both nodded eagerly, forgetting their new friend could not see, and Andrea continued, "She and Sir Roderick organized the Northoaks Companies in a big tin-foil collection for that same Association. And now he's getting the various clubs and churches in this district interested in the scheme. Lots of them are collecting furiously; in fact only the other day he was talking about approaching the Guides and Scouts about it. You'd be invaluable to him, for you could call regularly on all the club secretaries and collect their supplies in bulk, as well as making new contacts yourselves."

Chris and Bunny exchanged excited glances.

"S-Sandra's father knows Sir Roderick," said Bunny eagerly. "That's how we f-first heard about it." She hugged herself with glee. "When we've g-got our target, we're going to have a signed portrait of the Guide dog for our P-patrol corner."

An expression of comical surprise crossed Andrea's face.

"A signed portrait?" she asked. "Who'll sign it? The dog?"

Bunny looked taken aback, and Chris explained with a chuckle, "She means a framed portrait." She thought for a moment, and then said, "If Sir Roderick's looking for Guides to help him, should we call on him this evening and put the Poppies at his disposal? We've got bikes, and we could go wherever he wanted to send us."

Before Andrea could reply, Bunny said anxiously, "We'd still have the money c-credited to the *Poppies*' Guide Dog, wouldn't we?"

Andrea smiled reassuringly at her. "Of course, my dear! You both go and see him this evening, and I'll write him a follow-up letter. Yes, I *can* write," she added, sensing their surprise. "I use a writing frame with elastic guide lines. Sir Roderick's quite used to receiving little notes from me!"

The Guides' excitement was almost at boiling point by this time, and questions came tumbling from them both.

"What's Sir Roderick like?" was Chris's final question. She was wondering if she and Bunny would find him very formidable.

Andrea's expressive face lighted up.

"He's a dear," she said warmly. "He's been almost like a father to me, over the years I've known him. It was he who was responsible for getting my Guide Dog for me. More important still, it was Sir Roderick who introduced me to the best Guide of all!"

Both her visitors looked puzzled and, sensing this, Andrea's lips curved into a little smile.

"To be an out-and-out Guide you need to *have* a Guide," she explained. "Sir Roderick taught me that, and he gave me a promise from the Bible, to be my watchword: *He* (that means God) *will be our guide even unto death.* I was in the Extensions when I was younger, and it's a case of 'Once a Guide, always a Guide'," she added with a smile.

She stood up with an easy, graceful movement, and Judy sprang to the alert. "I think you should go to Sir Roderick at once. Tell him I sent you, and that he'll be receiving a note from me to-morrow; and don't forget to come and see me again soon, will you? I shall be eager to hear how you get on. In fact, come whenever you like! You'll always be sure of a welcome."

"We will, thank you," Chris told her with alacrity.

As they left the cottage a few moments later the P.L. glanced at her watch. It would only take about ten minutes to get to *The Hollies*. They should be there by a quarter past seven, she decided.

Actually, it was rather before that when they turned the final corner and found themselves within a few feet of the big gates. The soft purring of an engine reached their ears, and almost immediately a car came backing slowly out of the drive.

The Poppies exchanged tragic glances. Was Sir Roderick going out at the very moment of their arrival?

CHAPTER 6

ADVENTURE AT 'THE HOLLIES'

As Chris and Bunny came to a halt, uncertain what to do next, a tiny boy toddled into view. Standing directly in the path of the oncoming car, unconscious of the wheels rolling relentlessly towards him, he eyed the Poppies solemnly, his finger in his mouth.

Bunny screamed, and in that same moment Chris acted. She threw herself forward, pushed the tiny form to safety, and fell spread-eagled on the gravelled path, flung there by the wing of the big car.

For a few moments everything seemed to be spinning. Then the P.L. felt herself lifted by a pair of strong arms and lowered gently on to the step of the now stationary car. Gradually the scene got into focus again, and she found herself gazing up into a pair of anxious, blue eyes in a kindly, handsome face which had gone pale under its tan.

In the distance, a yelling little toddler was being hugged and scolded in turn by a fair-haired young woman, while an older woman, very like Sir

Roderick in appearance, was running from the house to the scene of the accident.

"Are you hurt?" Sir Roderick asked Chris anxiously. "What on earth happened?"

Chris smiled a trifle shakily.

"No, I'm all right, thank you," she said. "I just pushed the little boy out of the way of your car. You were backing straight into him."

A horrified expression crossed Sir Roderick's face.

"Thank God you had the presence of mind to act promptly," he said, pushing his hand through his thick, wavy hair. "I should never have forgiven myself if anything had happened to my little grandson; and certainly his mother would never have forgiven me!" he added ruefully. "I'm more grateful to you than I can say! Are you sure you're not hurt?"

"Bring her indoors, Rod," his sister interrupted him briskly. "A cup of tea is what she needs." She turned to Bunny who was hovering uncertainly in the background, her pointed little face completely bereft of colour. "You look as if you need treatment for shock too, child! We'll see if the housekeeper can produce a second cup."

She slipped her hand under Chris's elbow, and the Patrol Leader was only too thankful for the little support.

By the time she and Bunny had drunk the hot, sweet tea, however, and Chris's grazed hands and knees had been bathed, they were both looking and feeling more themselves.

"Actually, we were coming to see you," Chris told Sir Roderick, to his obvious surprise. "But aren't we keeping you? You seemed to be going out."

Sir Roderick glanced at his watch. "I was, as it happened, but it's too late now. It doesn't matter very much. Tell me what you came to see me about. If it's something I can help you with, I'll be only too glad. I owe you a debt I can never discharge. If you hadn't happened to appear at that moment . . ."

He broke off with an involuntary little shudder, and then added: "I mustn't say you *happened* to appear, though. Things like that are not a matter of luck. It was Providence."

"You mean that God t-timed our visit?" asked Bunny eagerly. "Miss Whitfield told us when to come. God m-must have guided her. She told us about her w-watchword: *He will be our guide even unto death.*"

"You know Andrea?" Sir Roderick exchanged glances with his sister. "Yes, I'm quite sure God did guide her. She has learned to be very sensitive to His leading. But what made her send you to me?"

The Poppies promptly broke into a lively account of their new Patrol Service and Andrea's suggestion about his own possible part in it, each taking up the story in turn.

"So we've come to put the Poppies at your service, if you'd like to use us," finished Chris simply.

Sir Roderick brought his fist down on the arm of his chair.

"That's the best news I've heard in weeks," he declared. "I can give you the addresses right away of eight or nine people who'll be glad if you'd collect a bulk supply from them each month. Club Leaders and Secretaries, you know. And I can put you in touch with quite a few business acquaintances of mine whose families have taken up tin-foil collecting with enthusiasm since I came to live in these parts. Have you thought what you're going to name your puppy, by the way? Now that you're really getting organized, you might write to the headquarters of the Association about it."

"The puppy's almost certain to be a lady," put in his sister. "Ninety per cent of the Guide Dogs are. You'll have to call a Patrol meeting to make the big decision," she added with a little smile.

Chris nodded seriously.

"We'll make it the first item on our agenda," she told her.

The next quarter of an hour passed quickly as the two Poppies jotted down addresses at Sir Roderick's dictation and made copious notes. Then they both rose to leave.

"I've another idea at the back of my mind that I think will appeal to you," said Sir Roderick, as he walked with them to the door. "Just for the present, though, I'm keeping it a secret!"

He held out his hand and enveloped Chris's in a warm clasp. "I shan't easily forget what you did this evening," he told her quietly.

Miss Carson held out her left hand, and both Guides saluted her as they gripped it in turn. Then they were walking quickly together down the drive, feeling little the worse for their adventure on arrival.

"Hallo!" called an astonished voice as they reached the road, and the Fuchsia Patrol Leader jumped off her bike, followed closely by her Second. "Moving in high society, aren't we?" she added with a chuckle. "I didn't know you knew the Carsons."

Chris grinned.

"We didn't till this evening," she admitted.

"Why are you both wearing your uniforms, Clare?"

"We might ask you the same question," the P.L. retorted. "Actually, Rose and I have been out on our Patrol Service—washing up after fifty children! Not exactly a glamorous form of service, admittedly, but we heard that the Children's Home had sent out an S.O.S. for helpers. Captain was rather pleased," she added modestly. "We're doing it in pairs three nights a week, this being our first."

"We've been on our Patrol Service, too," Bunny told her eagerly. "It was f-fun."

The Fuchsias propped their bikes against the wall and prepared for a good chat. There was nothing the Guides liked so much as 'talking shop'.

"My!" said Clare, when the Poppies' account of their evening's activities (omitting the car incident) came to an end; and there was the least trace of envy in her grey eyes.

"But we think *your* Service is more special in a way," said Chris generously.

Rose reached for her handlebars.

"I'll have to be getting on," she said reluctantly. "I've got to be home before eight. I suppose you don't know what the Pansies are doing for their Service? It's something to do with Sunshine

Boxes, whatever they may be. But that's all I could gather."

Chris could offer no enlightenment.

"I've no idea," she said regretfully—little guessing the dramatic way in which the question was soon to be answered.

CHAPTER 7

OUT OF THE STORM

"PENELOPE!" Chris jumped off her bike and hurried towards the Pansy Patrol Leader, who was sitting at the roadside, ruefully inspecting a cut knee. At her side lay her bike, the front wheel still revolving and the handlebars wrenched out of position.

It was the Saturday afternoon following the adventure at *The Hollies* and Chris had set out for a cycle ride in the country. The day was hot and oppressive, and she had felt an urge to get right away from the town. She had not long left the last lamp-post behind and turned into a country road, however, before she was halted by the plight of her fellow Patrol Leader.

Penelope smiled up at her a bit shakily. "I must have run over a stone or something. It made me wobble furiously, and I ran into that tree. I've got my pocket first aid outfit on me, if you could fish it out."

Chris helped her to a fallen tree-trunk nearby.

"Good thing you were in uniform," she commented, as she set to work on the damaged knee, "otherwise you probably wouldn't have had it with you. You're not out Guiding, though, are you?"

Penelope nodded. "In a way. I'm taking the Pansies' Sunshine Box out to the Ashby Memorial Hospital—for our Patrol Service. At least, *I was*. It doesn't look as if I'll make it, now."

Chris paused in her ministrations.

"You could finish the journey on *my* bike," she offered.

She pressed the bandaged knee as she spoke, and Penelope gave an involuntary little gasp of pain.

"I don't think I *can* cycle," she said unhappily. "It's not that I'm funking it, but the cut's exactly where I bend my knee to pedal!"

The Poppy P.L. nodded quickly.

"You can't go on; I can see that," she agreed at once. "If you can tell me about this—Sunshine Box, did you call it?—perhaps I can take over for you. I'm going right past the hospital."

"Oh, would you really?" Penelope's face lighted up. "It will be all right if you just hand it in to the porter at the lodge. I was going to ask if I could take it to an old lady of 90 in the Elizabeth Anderson Ward, but you needn't do that. The porter will see that Gran gets it. Do you know what a Sunshine Box is, by the way?"

Chris put away the first aid outfit and settled herself on the log beside Penelope.

"No—what is it?" she asked with interest, and the Pansy P.L. explained that it was a box containing seven small gifts for a hospital patient, each wrapped separately in pretty, coloured paper and marked with the day of the week on which it was to be opened.

"We're going to try to make one box every month, out of our Patrol funds, for different patients," she concluded.

"What a grand idea!" Chris exclaimed appreciatively. "It means that the patient can begin every day with a surprise! I think it's a splendid kind of Patrol Service. What's in Gran's box?"

Penelope thought for a moment and then began listing the items: "A tablet of scented soap and a face flannel, a little bottle of lavender water, three pretty hankies, a box of Notelets and a book of postage stamps, a little illustrated John's Gospel—to be opened on the Sunday—and a couple more things which I've forgotten for the moment."

"Sounds lovely!" Chris said, with a beaming smile. "I haven't heard of that idea before."

"I've underlined John, chapter 14, verses 1 and 2, in the Gospel," Penelope told her. "I thought it would be sort of comforting to her, as she's so old."

As Chris looked blank, Penelope added: "It's that nice bit about the many mansions, you know.

'Let not your heart be troubled: ye believe in God, believe also in me. In my Father's house are many mansions: if it were not so, I would have told you. I go to prepare a place for you.' I know that bit off by heart."

Chris looked at her curiously. "You know quite a lot of Bible passages off by heart, don't you?"

"Well, quite a few. My favourites, anyway. There's a little Psalm I rather like, about The Person God Loves, and one verse in particular could be about a Guide or Scout. It says he makes a promise and doesn't go back on it whatever the consequences. That's like the first Scout and Guide Law, isn't it? It's in Psalm 15. Don't you ever read the Bible yourself?"

"No, not really," Chris admitted. She stood up. "I think I'd better be going on with your Sunshine Box, Pen. I don't like the look of the sky. How will you manage about getting home?"

"Oh, I'll limp along all right," Penelope told her cheerfully. "The bike's not heavy to push. Thanks a lot for what you're doing. The box will be a nice surprise for Gran. She's not expecting it. I hope the porter will take it to her as soon as you hand it in."

"I'll ask him to," Chris promised.

She found the porter most friendly when she arrived a few minutes later.

"Feels like a storm coming up," he greeted her as she pushed her bike through the gates. "You're not wanting to visit anyone, are you? Visiting time is not till this evening, unless you've had special permission?"

The girl shook her head. "No, thanks, but I'd be awfully glad if someone could take this box to a patient. It's for Gran in the Elizabeth Anderson Ward."

Sensing his interest, she gave him a lively account of the Pansies' Good Deed that nearly didn't come off. He was immediately sympathetic.

"I'll see Gran has it at once," he promised, and Chris put it gratefully into his hands.

As she jumped on her bike again, the first spots of heavy rain fell, followed a few minutes later by a loud clap of thunder. Chris turned up the collar of her light plastic mackintosh and bent over the pedals, but before she had covered more than a few yards the rain was pouring down in torrents. There was another angry clap; then, almost without a pause, came more flashes of lightning accompanied by angry peals of thunder.

Through the deluge, Chris could just see a cottage a little distance ahead. It was impossible to go much farther. She covered the intervening distance with a desperate burst of speed, propped her cycle against the wall, and knocked urgently on the door. It was opened almost immediately, and anxious hands pulled her inside. Then the door was closed behind her with a bang, and she found herself gazing into the thin, kindly face of a middle-aged woman who was dressed in outdoor attire.

"You poor lamb; you're drenched!" exclaimed the cottager, leading her into the little living-room. "Here, take off your wet mackintosh, and give me your shoes and stockings. I'll dry them for you on the kitchen stove."

She slipped off her outdoor attire as she spoke, and then found Chris a pair of warm, felt shoes.

"I'm afraid I've dripped all over your floor," the girl apologized. "It came on so suddenly. I'd just left the hospital and I thought I might get home before the storm really broke, but——"

"Just left the hospital, had you?" Mrs. Griggs interrupted her. "And I was just about to go there! I wanted to leave a parcel for my old mother; just a little surprise for her, as I can't get along in the visiting half-hour tonight. Gran, they all call her. She's turned ninety, and a little surprise now and then does a lot to cheer her up."

Chris dried her face on the towel Mrs. Griggs had handed to her, and asked eagerly, "Is she in the Elizabeth Anderson Ward?"

Mrs. Griggs nodded, obviously surprised at the

girl's knowledge, and Chris went on with a rush, "Then you needn't worry about not getting your surprise to her. I've just taken one for her myself!"

In the sudden flash of lightning that illuminated the dim room, she saw the astonishment in Mrs. Griggs' face, and for the second time that afternoon she launched into an account of the Pansies' Patrol Service and the accident to their Leader, ending with her delivery of the box to the porter's lodge.

Mrs. Griggs' face was one big beam.

"Well, I never!" was all she could say. She took the damp towel from Chris, and added, "Do let me make you a cup of tea, Miss. One good turn deserves another, and it may save you from getting a nasty chill."

Chris has been about to refuse, but seeing the wisdom of the last remark she decided to accept gratefully.

As they drank the cheering brew, chatting about Gran and her disabilities, the thunder gradually became more distant.

"The rain's leaving off now," announced Mrs. Griggs at last. "You'll be able to make a dash for it in a minute or two, I think. Your poor bicycle must be quite drowned, but I've no shed to put it in."

Chris laughed.

"The rain won't hurt it. It's not the first time it's been out in a deluge," she assured the cottager. "Let me take the cups through to the kitchen for you and wash them up. It's the least I can do."

Mrs. Griggs started to protest, but Chris had already laid hands on them. As she entered the little kitchen an exclamation escaped her lips. On the draining board was a paper carrier filled to capacity with precious milk-bottle tops!

CHAPTER 8

AN ENJOYABLE VISIT

TEN minutes later, Chris was cycling happily along the wet, sweet-smelling lanes, the carrier full of tin-foil bulging out of her cycle bag.

Mrs. Griggs had been only too thankful to part with it, having collected the bottle tops over a period of months because she had a vague idea that they could be 'sold for charity' and it seemed wrong to throw them away.

As Chris coasted downhill towards the town, she glanced at her watch. Her mother was not expecting her back just yet. She would call on Miss Whitfield and tell her the result of the visit to *The Hollies* earlier in the week!

Andrea welcomed her warmly when she arrived. She had been busy at her braille writer and several large sheets were stacked neatly beside her. But she was not at all put out at being disturbed: in fact she seemed delighted to have Chris with her.

"You must peep into my bedroom," she said. "This is only a wee cottage. Two rooms down and two up. My landlady lives upstairs, and we share the kitchen. She's very kind to me."

Chris followed her into the cosy, little bedroom, with its easy chair in one corner and small, springy bed with gay bedspread. The late afternoon sun, pouring in through the gaily curtained window, lighted up a scroll on the wall.

Andrea seemed to sense at what her guest was looking.

"You like it?" she asked. "It's beautifully hand-lettered, I'm told! Miss Carson had it done especially for my wall. It's from Isaiah. Read it aloud, will you? I never tire of hearing it."

And Chris obediently read: "*I will bring the blind by a way that they knew not; I will lead them in paths that they have not known: I will make darkness light before them, and crooked things straight. These things will I do unto them, and not forsake them.* Oh, Miss Whitfield, it's lovely!" she added sincerely.

Andrea smiled, obviously pleased by the P.L.'s appreciation, as she led her back into the sitting-room.

"Will you give me a lesson on your braille machine some time?" Chris asked her shyly, dropping into a chair. "I want to tackle the Friend to the Blind badge, later on, if I can. You have to be able to transcribe from print, with not more than 10 errors, three large sheets of braille; and you have to read by sight or touch, Grade 1 braille—whatever that may be!—interlined and written on both sides. Is braille very hard?"

Andrea considered this.

"I wouldn't call it easy," she admitted, "but you could pick it up if you were really willing to stick at it. You won't do it in a week, though!" she added with a smile. "Incidentally, Sir Roderick's been appointed Examiner for the Scouts and Guides in this district: for that particular test, I mean. How did you get on when you went to visit him?"

"That's what I really came to tell you about," Chris told her. "His sister was there, and we all got on splendidly together."

She related in detail the story of the visit, omitting only her rescue of his little grandson from certain tragedy.

Andrea listened intently, her face alight with interest.

"I thought he'd be pleased," she said with satisfaction. "And you've been able to compile a splendid, long list of regular suppliers, into the bargain!"

"We've written to The Guide Dogs for the Blind Association, too," Chris told her eagerly, "and we've chosen a name for the Poppies' Guide Dog. She's to be *Kim*! Sandra's given us some photographs of Guide Dogs in action. One's taking a blind woman across a road, in traffic, and another's leading her owner around an obstacle on the pavement. They're lovely dogs!"

"They certainly are," agreed Andrea with feeling. "I don't know what I'd do without Judy, now." She bent to give the dog an affectionate pat. "She's perfectly trained. When we're out together she stops at every kerb, and waits for the command to cross. And if I've given the command and it's not safe to cross, she stays on the pavement till the road is clear, before leading me over."

"But what happens if you meet traffic halfway across?" asked Chris anxiously.

Andrea smiled. "She stops and waits till it's safe to continue. Then she carries on again without any command. Do you know the four commands a Guide Dog has to learn?"

"*Forward! Right! Left!* and *Sit!*" said Chris promptly. "We've been studying it all up, because of Kim. In fact, Bunny's been trying them out on her mongrel pup. But she didn't have much success! When she said *Right!* he just rolled on his back and waved his paws in the air!"

Sudden laughter bubbled from them both at the picture conjured up. Then Chris asked doubtfully, "What I can't understand is how a dog knows where to find, say, the Post Office, if that's where you want to go?"

Andrea chuckled. "She doesn't, first go off. The owner has to give the necessary commands till they reach it. But after the dog has been there a few times it's only necessary to say 'Post Office' and she'll lead her owner there without further directions. That's all I have to say to Judy, anyway! You must come out with us both one day and watch her at work. You'd be interested, I think."

"I'd love to," said Chris at once. "Did you have to go away and train with her before you had her home with you?"

Andrea nodded vigorously.

"I certainly did," she assured her. "We had a whole month together at a Training Centre. I needed to learn how to work with her, how to feel Judy's movements through the harness, and know what those movements meant. I had to be able to recognize the guidance, you see, as well as learning to have faith in my four-footed guide. And that meant spending time with her every day."

Before Chris could reply, she added thoughtfully, "It's rather like that with spiritual things, too. I think I told you my special watchword the other day: *He (God) will be our guide even unto death.* To be able to recognize His guidance, we need to spend time alone with Him every day, listening to His voice speaking to us through the Bible."

Chris nodded uncertainly, forgetting for the moment that Andrea couldn't see the gesture.

Her eyes strayed around the room.

"You've got a Bible on your bookshelf, but it's in ordinary print, not braille," she commented with surprise.

"And an ordinary copy of *The Story of My Life* by Helen Keller, next door to it," added Andrea, with a little smile. "They're for my friends to read to me. Have you ever read Helen Keller's life story, by the way? It's an amazing one."

Chris shook her head. "No, but I'd like to read it aloud to you some time—like your other friends," she said shyly.

Her eyes strayed to the braille clock on the mantelpiece and she jumped to her feet. "I think I'd better be going now, Miss Whitfield, but I'll come again soon. I like coming," she added naïvely.

Andrea and Judy accompanied her to the door, and Chris leapt nimbly on to her bike on the roadway outside. The sky had become a cloudless blue, and close by, a blackbird—bathed in golden sunshine—sang with joyful abandon. The storm was over.

As she pedalled home, Andrea's watchword suddenly ran through Chris's mind, followed by the casual little remark she had made at their first meeting: "To be an out-and-out Guide you need to *have* a Guide." She wished she'd asked her to enlarge a bit on the subject, she decided, a little wistfully. But perhaps they'd be together again before long, and she would have another opportunity.

CHAPTER 9

A SURPRISE FOR CHRIS

"SAFE home!" said Captain cheerfully, as eighteen sun-tanned Guides and two Guiders jumped nimbly from a hired lorry, and began unloading their camp equipment into the Guide Hut.

It was the Saturday following Chris's visit to Andrea, and Captain and Lieutenant had taken the Company for a Day Camp, as a preliminary to their ten days under canvas next summer.

Bunny was limping noticeably, but she was in excellent spirits. It had been the loveliest day of the summer, she declared. She had never been to camp before, and her green eyes had glowed with excitement as Captain and Lieutenant showed the Guides how to pitch tents, build a cooking fire, make camp gadgets, and a host of other things.

The smallest Poppy had distinguished herself when they played a woodcraft game called Tree Detectives, and her delight had known no bounds when she learned that her own Patrol had been chosen as Cooks and were to cook the camp dinner on a real wood fire! The only snag had been the milk. She had begged to be allowed to collect it from the farmer—and tripping over one of the store-tent guy lines on her return journey, had spilled the lot! Happily, Captain had quickly forgiven her, and now all she had to show for it was a limp.

A treasure hunt in an orchard had been great fun in the afternoon, and this had been followed by more campcraft instruction. Later, they had all had tea around the blazing camp fire, with a lively sing-song to follow, finishing up with a quiet talk from Captain and a little prayer from Lieutenant.

And now, with the evening still young, they were safely back at their hut, unloading their kit, with Bunny enthusiastically checking the tent pegs and mallets.

"Is my young sister around?" an amused, masculine voice broke into the scene of activity, and Chris extricated herself from a mass of canvas screening to see her brother at the hut door.

"Colin!" she exclaimed in surprise.

"Yes, me," he grinned. "Sir Roderick phoned about half an hour ago to ask if you'd go round to *The Hollies* this evening. It seems he's got a big surprise for you, so I thought I'd better see if you'd returned from your day's spree!"

"Day Camp—not day's spree," Chris automatically corrected him.

Captain paused in her task of collecting up groundsheets.

"I should leave everything and go," she said. "The rest of us will see the job through."

Chris hesitated, torn between a sense of duty towards the Guides, who were still struggling with the heavy equipment, and a longing to discover the nature of the surprise in store for her. Then:

"Thanks, Captain," she said gratefully. And with a smart salute she turned on her heel.

"I feel an awful fright," she told Colin as they fell into step together. "I spilt gravy down my camp overall when we were serving up the dinner, and I found Bunny squatting on my beret during the camp-fire sing-song! I'll have to change before I cycle round to *The Hollies*."

Colin eyed her critically.

"A wash wouldn't be a bad idea, either," he returned candidly. "The sun's made your nose peel, but I don't suppose you can do much about that!"

Chris joined in his chuckle, and the about journey home passed quickly as she entertained him with some of the highlights of the day, including Bunny's misadventure with the milk.

Half an hour later a spack-and-span Chris presented herself at *The Hollies*.

Miss Carson, who had been picking flowers from

the beds bordering the drive, straightened her back and welcomed her with a warm smile.

"Come in, my dear child. My brother's got something to show you! I'll let you into the house with my key. He's in his study, I believe."

As she reached out a hand towards the door, it opened—to reveal a sight which made Chris gasp.

A tiny, curly-headed boy stood framed in the doorway, his arm lightly around the neck of a huge St. Bernard dog who stood quietly beside him. Behind them, she could see the smiling face of Sir Roderick.

"Oh, the lovely creature!" she cried. "Is he yours, Sir Roderick?"

He smiled at her exclamation of delight.

"My grandson, as you know"—he introduced the child—"but not my dog! I'm minding him for my son, this little fellow's daddy. He's gone to South Africa for a few months. I thought you'd like the dog," he added, with satisfaction.

He gently lifted the little boy out of the way, so that Chris might have a clearer view of the St. Bernard. What she saw made her eyes open still wider. On the back of the massive dog was a coat bearing the lettering GUIDE DOGS FOR THE BLIND ASSOCIATION. And above the wording was a single, scarlet flower, made from felt. It was the Poppy Patrol emblem!

Sir Roderick laughed at her eager, half-puzzled expression; then he shepherded her into his study.

"That's why I sent for you," he explained. "In fact, it's what I had in mind when I told you, on the night you saved my grandson's life, that I had an idea at the back of my mind that I thought would appeal to you."

He motioned her into a seat and took one opposite her. "I got the idea from one of the Association's handbooks, where there was a photo of a St. Bernard collecting money for Guide Dogs. I realized that the only way in which I could repay you in some small measure for what you did that night, was by helping you and your Patrol to realize your big ambition."

He called the dog to him and pointed to a pair of small, strong straps which were slotted through the lettered coat.

Chris looked at him enquiringly.

"The collecting box fastens on there," he said, "and I shall be very surprised if this big fellow doesn't prove a great attraction at the Summer Fête next month, and at one or two other events I have in mind: the Band Contest, for example, and the Horticultural Show."

The P.L.'s face was one big smile.

"Will the Poppies be in charge of him?" she asked.

"The Poppies and my grandson," Sir Roderick told her solemnly. "Little Paul refuses to let the dog—Bernie, he calls him!—out of his sight, and Bernie's just as devoted to Paul. But that will probably add to the attraction at those public gatherings. The two make rather a picture together, don't they? You noticed that as you came in. I've obtained my son's consent, of course. He was only too eager to co-operate when he heard how you'd saved his son from an untimely end!"

Miss Carson put her head round the door.

"How did our young friend receive the news?" she enquired with a broad smile.

"I think it's wonderful!" Chris exclaimed, without giving Sir Roderick time to reply. "We shall raise simply *pounds* for our dog, Kim. Far more than with the tin-foil."

Sir Roderick stood up.

"Don't despise the work you are doing," he said seriously. "It was partly because you've proved faithful over that humble job that I felt encouraged to give you this more spectacular one. You won't have to handle the money yourselves. I'll take charge of what you collect. It will have to be changed into a cheque, anyway. And I'll see that the sums are duly credited to the Poppies' fund for Kim. I suspect that your framed photo seems less distant than it did, young lady!"

Chris jumped to her feet.

"Oh, thank you, Sir Roderick," she said earnestly. "All the Poppies will be thrilled. It's the best surprise you could possibly have thought of."

As she jumped on her bike a few minutes later, a sudden thought came to her. She would ride round to Miss Whitfield and share the exciting news with her!

She looked at her watch, and her face fell. Perhaps, after all, she had better go straight home. But she would visit her blind friend as soon as she could, for she knew how delighted Andrea would be. As for the rest of the Patrol, they would be almost delirious with joy when she told them the great news!

CHAPTER 10

ANDREA EXPLAINS

"CHRIS! Do come in," Andrea greeted the Poppy P.L. when she arrived on her doorstep three evenings later. "I can feel you simply exuding excitement. Has something special happened?"

She led the way into the sitting-room as she spoke, and they both dropped into easy chairs, the faithful Judy, released from her white harness, taking up her position at Andrea's feet.

"I should just say it has!" Chris told her, and in a few sentences she described her visit to *The Hollies* on the previous Saturday and all that had happened there.

"I *am* glad," Andrea said sincerely. "The St. Bernard will help you tremendously towards your target. But I agree with Sir Roderick that you mustn't belittle the work you're already doing. How's it going, by the way?"

Chris's face light up.

"Splendidly!" she said. "In addition to the big haul we've been getting from the clubs and the regular calls we make at the different houses, we've contacted a restaurant, a canteen, and a snack bar. And they are all going to save their pie-cases and milk-bottle tops for us! Sandra's going to see if she can collect from the hospital kitchen, too, but of course they may want to keep their tin-foil to sell in bulk themselves. We're enjoying it tremendously, and I think Sir Roderick is pleased, too."

She sprawled her length luxuriously in the arm-chair, feeling thoroughly at home there.

"Why didn't you tell me about your rescue of his little grandson from the car wheels?" Andrea wanted to know. "It must have meant a tremendous lot to Sir Roderick. The little chap is the apple of his eye."

Chris coloured.

"Oh, it was nothing," she said uncomfortably. "Anyone would have done the same if they'd been on the spot." Hastily she changed the subject. "We had a super Day Camp last Saturday. The weather was perfect and we all got back looking like Red Indians. Would you be interested to hear about it?"

Andrea said an eager "Oh, please!" and the Poppy felt again the now-familiar sense of comradeship between them. She described the day's activities in detail. Then she spoke of the Guides' Own around the camp fire.

"It made a peaceful ending to the day," she said reminiscently. "Captain talked to us about the tenth Guide law: *A Guide is pure in thought, word, and deed.* She began by warning us that we couldn't live up to it in our own strength; we needed to ask God to help us. And for 'A Guide is pure in *word*' she quoted King David's prayer, 'Keep the door of my lips.'"

Andrea nodded, following with interest.

"Captain said it was just as important, too, for our eyes to be guarded," Chris continued; "and she told us to be careful what programmes we watched on television, and what books and magazines we read."

"Very wise," commented Andrea. "And what did she say about purity of *thought*?"

"Oh, she said that was awfully important, because if our thoughts were pure, our deeds would be, too! I can't remember all she said but she ended up by reading a bit from the New Testament, something about whatsoever things are true, and honest, and just, and pure, and lovely, '*think on these things*'."

"That's from Paul's Letter to the Philippians," said Andrea promptly, "and excellent advice it is, too. The Bible's more full of down-to-earth common-sense than any book I know."

There was a thoughtful little silence for a while;

then Chris said suddenly, "Penelope, our Fuchsia P.L., gave me a verse the other week, linking up with the first Guide Law. So that makes two. Is there a Bible verse for all of them, Miss Whitfield?"

Andrea's musical laugh rippled out.

"Not that I know of, but there quite well could be," she admitted. "You'll have to experiment with a concordance one day, and see!"

Judy gave a prodigous yawn, obviously bored by the conversation, and Chris bent down and stroked her. She was rewarded by a friendly lick! After a moment she said, "I've been thinking a lot about something you said a little while ago, that to be an out-and-out Guide we need to *have* a Guide, and of your watchword, *He will be our guide even unto death*. But what I don't understand is this: if He's *my* Guide, and I'm keen to be an out-and-out Guide, why do I keep slipping up? This morning I was bad-tempered and awfully rude to Mummy, because I got out of bed the wrong side. I was terribly sorry afterwards."

Andrea smiled sympathetically. Then she said, "Have you ever opened your heart to the Lord Jesus, Chris?"

The girl didn't reply at once; she was too taken aback. And Andrea went on, "I expect you know the famous picture, by Holman Hunt, called *The*

Light of the World; there's a beautiful reproduction of it in St. Paul's Cathedral."

"I've seen a picture postcard of it," Chris told her, hesitantly, "but I didn't understand it very well."

"It portrays the Lord Jesus Christ knocking on the door of the human heart," Andrea explained, "and I once heard an interesting little story about it. A guide was showing a party of tourists over St. Paul's Cathedral, and when he reached the place where the picture hung he said in a loud, impressive voice, 'The original of that picture, ladies and gentlemen, was sold for £5,000!' There was an awed little silence. Then a visitor to the Cathedral, who was standing near by, said quietly, 'The *real* Original of that picture, ladies and gentlemen, was sold for 30 pieces of silver.'"

Chris's face was very serious.

"Judas Iscariot did it," she said slowly. "He sold Him for the price of a slave. Our minister preached about it at Easter. But he said that Jesus gave His life willingly—because He loved us."

"He loved us and gave Himself for us," said Andrea, her face alight with gratitude and love.

"*He died that we might be forgiven,*
He died to make us good,
That we might go at last to heaven,
Saved by His precious blood,

just as the hymn says. But God brought Him back to life again, and He's knocking on the door of *your* heart, Chris—if you haven't already let Him in."

"I haven't," Chris admitted. "Nobody's ever explained it to me like that before."

She lapsed into silence, thinking deeply.

"You mentioned my watchword just now," Andrea said.

The P.L. looked at her eagerly, and she went on, "God's own children can turn confidently to Him and receive guidance at any moment of the day or night."

Chris gazed at her in astonishment. "His children? But I thought we were *all* God's children. He made us all, didn't He?"

"Yes, but that makes Him our Creator, not our Father," Andrea pointed out logically. "Nobody is *born* a Christian! Reach down my Bible from the bookshelf, there's a dear, and find the first chapter of St. John's Gospel, verse 12."

Chris obediently reached for the volume and leafed through its pages.

"What does it say?" Andrea prompted her, and she read aloud, "As many as received him, to them gave he power to become the sons of God."

"The marginal reading puts it even more clearly: *As many as received him, to them gave he the right to become children of God,*" Andrea quoted. "But did you notice the conditions? *As many as received him.* That means receiving the Lord Jesus into our hearts as our Saviour, for it applies today as much as it did when He was on earth."

Chris considered this for some moments. Then she said slowly, "Jesus is much bigger than I am, isn't He?"

Andrea nodded her agreement, and Chris went on, groping for words, "So if I asked Him into my heart, to live inside me, everyone would see Him there."

Her blind friend's face was illuminated by a sudden, radiant smile.

"That's quite true," she agreed. "But it wouldn't be anything to be ashamed of. Quite the reverse, in fact! They'd simply see Him in your life, in your *really* living out the Guide Law."

Chris's face broke into a beaming smile that was almost a reflection of Andrea's. Here was the answer to her problem at last.

"And how do I receive Him?" she asked eagerly.

"If I were you," said Andrea quietly, "I think I'd simply kneel by my bedside and say to Him, 'Please forgive my sins, Lord Jesus, and come into my heart to live.' He will do that so gladly, for He has said that if anyone opens the door He will come in, and He never breaks His word."

Chris nodded vigorously.

"I'll do it when I say my prayers tonight," she said with conviction.

A tap on the sitting-room door interrupted their conversation, and Andrea's landlady appeared in the doorway, carrying a tray laden with cups, saucers, plates, a jug of coffee, and a plate of sandwiches.

"Oh, Mrs. Kirby, how kind of you!" said Andrea warmly, hearing the rattle of the cups, and she held out her hands for the tray. "She always does that when I have a visitor," she told Chris, as the door closed behind the motherly soul. "I wonder if you'd like to pour out the coffee for us? It smells delicious."

Chris reached for the jug, and soon they were enjoying the refreshment. Judy was not forgotten, either!

A sudden thought struck the P.L. as the dog lapped up her share of the coffee.

"Miss Whitfield, you don't think we're putting all this enthusiasm into collecting tin-foil just to try to reach our target and have a framed picture for the Patrol Corner, do you?" she asked anxiously. "It's because we honestly do want to try to help someone to have a dog like Judy and be able to live a much happier sort of life."

Andrea reached out and gripped her hand. "I do realize that, my dear, and so does Sir Roderick. He was here today and he talked about you. It was he, of course, who told me how you saved little Paul's life. We talked of Helen Keller too, and he read me some of my favourite extracts from her book, *The Story of My Life*. I never tire of hearing them; they're so full of her joy of living."

Chris was at once interested.

"I'd like to read some of them to you myself," she said eagerly.

"I think you'd enjoy it," Andrea told her. "She wrote the book when she was a young woman, and, as she describes the thrills of tobogganing and her love of rowing, swimming, canoeing, and horse-riding, the reader almost forgets that she's been blind and deaf ever since she was twenty months old! She's devoted the past fifty years of her life to lecturing in almost all parts of the world and to writing books to interest people in the welfare of the blind and deaf. If you've a few minutes to spare before you go, you could read to me now, Chris! You'd like the account of her first experience of the sea, I think."

Nothing loath, Chris took down the paper-backed volume and turned the pages till she came to the incident. Then, while Andrea lay back relaxed in her chair, she read aloud to her.

The description was vivid: first, the blind child's plunge into the cool water whose buoyancy filled her with quivering joy, then the change to terror as her foot struck against a rock and the water rushed over her head; her hopeless attempt to get support from the seaweed which the waves flung in her face, and finally her overwhelming relief when, as if weary of its new toy, the sea thrust her back on to the shore and she found herself clasped in her teacher's arms.

" 'Oh, the comfort of it!' " Chris read on. " 'As soon as I had recovered from my panic sufficiently to say anything, I demanded: *Who put salt in the water?*' "

Andrea and Chris burst into spontaneous laughter at the ingenuous question. Then Chris said thoughtfully, "She's a good, descriptive writer, isn't she? I'm going to study her style as I read the book to you, because I want to be an author when I grow up. What a pity Guides weren't invented when Miss Keller was a girl. She'd have loved it all!"

She put down the book reluctantly. It would have been fun to stay and read on, but there was her homework to be finished.

"I'm so glad you came," Andrea told her warmly,

as she and Judy saw her off a minute or two later. "I *have* enjoyed your visit."

"So have I," responded Chris, and added shyly, "I won't forget what I'm going to do before I go to bed tonight, Miss Whitfield. Thank you for explaining it to me!"

Then she jumped on her bike and pedalled swiftly away.

CHAPTER II

BABY SNATCHER!

THE next few weeks seemed to Chris to fly past on wings, packed as they were with Guide and school activities; and certainly they were the happiest she had known.

Ever since the night she had kneeled at her bedside to receive Jesus into her heart, after her chat with Andrea, something inside her had been singing. She still had problems, but she had learned to take them to God in prayer, and she was rapidly discovering for herself the truth of Andrea's own watchword: *He will be our guide even unto death.*

The rest of the Poppies were finding life equally busy. If they had imagined they had only to sit back and watch the coins fall into Bernie's collecting box they soon found they were mistaken, for Miss Carson phoned through one night to tell Chris that her brother was relying on the Patrol to help organize the children's sports at the Summer Fête.

Similarly, at the County Band Contest, which followed a week later in the bandstand of the park, the Poppies found themselves rushed off their feet at the refreshment tent; and at the Horticultural Show they were responsible for manning the washing-up tent. But it was all good fun—and just as well that the Poppies shouldn't get their Guide Dog gifts without some effort, as Captain remarked with a smile when she was approached for permission to wear uniform on the job.

As for Bernie and little Paul, the appeal they made, as they wove in and out of the crowds on all three occasions, was such that hearts and purses were opened on all sides.

The six Poppies took turns during their off-duty periods to supervise the pair, and they beamed with delight as the people thronged round them.

"I should think we've got close on a hundred pounds altogether," Chris confided to her mother when she got home from the Horticultural show. "Ever so many people put in shillings and half-crowns this time. Sir Roderick's going to phone me on Monday to let me know the total."

When the phone call came, it nearly took Chris's breath away. The Guide Dog proceeds for the three big events was £142 10*s.* 7*d.*

"Oh, Mums!" she exclaimed, as she replaced the receiver. "Isn't it just too wonderful for words? It's more than half the cost of training Kim and her owner. And we've filled two sacks with tin-foil as well! I'm going shopping with Bunny on Saturday to buy strong tie-on labels ready for the railway to collect the sacks. That'll be another 75*s.* to be credited to the Poppies, because it's worth £75 a ton."

Her mother smiled at her enthusiasm.

"You've done splendidly, all of you," she said warmly. "But you'll have to give up your street collections of tin-foil soon. The evenings are already drawing in, and in a week or two it'll be quite dark at night. I can't see Bunny's parents letting her continue after the end of this month, anyway."

Chris's face fell. Then it brightened again. "Never mind. I expect we'll think up some other ways of raising money for the Poppies' Guide Dog fund. I know! I'll give them 2*s.* each from Patrol funds, and we'll see if we can each turn our 2*s.* into £1, using every method of trading we can think of. We mustn't slacken off now that we're doing so well!"

Mrs. Temple's prediction about Bunny proved only too true, for when the youngest Poppy met the P.L. on the following Saturday morning she wore a very woebegone expression.

"Mummy says I've to stop the t-tin-foil collection when we put the clock back, at the end of official summer t-time," she said dismally.

"I think we'd all better stop our evening outings then," Chris told her, as they fell into step together. "Except for visits to the club secretaries and restaurants, I mean. We can fit those in on Saturdays. But I've thought up another idea for raising funds. I'm going to tell the Patrol about it at our next meeting. Have you got the money I gave you for the labels? We're nearly at the shop."

Bunny dived into her blazer pocket and produced a shilling.

"Shall we——" she began, but Chris cut her short.

"Bunny!" she said urgently. "I think I've just seen a woman snatch a baby from somebody's pram, outside the grocers. Look! See that woman in blue, walking quickly up the street with a baby in her arms? Well, she wasn't the one who left the pram outside the shop!"

"But the b-baby's not screaming," objected Bunny. "P'raps the woman's a friend."

Chris thought quickly.

"We mustn't take any chances," she said crisply. "Some babies will go to anybody. Here, take this red pencil. Follow her and mark an arrow on the pavement every time she turns a corner. I'll wait for the pram-owner, and if she *has* lost her baby we'll be able to track it!"

Bunny grabbed the pencil and hurried after her

quarry, while Chris waited patiently beside the empty pram.

Merging with the crowd of shoppers, and taking cover in shop doorways now and then, Bunny was thankful for the gamekeeper-and-poacher games she had played with the other Poppies over the last weeks, in preparation for the section of the Second Class test which required that a Guide should stalk an animal or person for fifteen minutes. She found that she needed all her wits about her as she drew closer, for the baby-snatcher constantly gave quick little glances over her shoulder.

As the crowds thinned, the stalking was even more difficult, and Bunny had suddenly to become engrossed in the contents of a shop window more than once. At another point she hastily stooped to tie her shoe-lace.

When her quarry finally turned out of the shopping thoroughfare, Bunny's heart sank. How could she possibly continue without arousing suspicion? But this was not a Patrol game, she told herself grimly. It was the real thing. So, using every stalking device she could call to mind, she stuck gamely to her task.

Chris, meanwhile, had kept her vigil to good effect. After what seemed an endless time, the owner of the pram suddenly appeared in the shop doorway, laden with groceries. Her eyes widened with horror as she caught sight of the empty pram, but just as she opened her mouth to scream Chris caught her by the arm.

"Come quickly," she said. "I'll take you to your baby."

She spoke with quiet confidence, but her heart was beating uncomfortably. Had Bunny managed to keep the woman in blue, with her precious burden, in sight?

As the two hurried up the High Street, leaving the empty pram parked outside the shop, Chris briefly explained what she and Bunny had planned.

"Look—here's an arrow pointing off to the left," she added, as the distraught mother began demanding police help. "There's not a policeman in sight, and by the time we'd got to a call-box and dialled 999 we'd have lost all hope of catching up with them. There's another red arrow just there. My friend's leaving a clear trail."

They were running now, heedless of the curious stares of passers by. Through a maze of turnings the trail led then, and finally towards. . . .

"The park!" cried the mother. "That's where she's taken the poor little lamb. Listen!"

Chris obediently listened. Her ears were not attuned to the baby's cry as were his mother's, but even she caught the sudden, fretful sound. In a flash the young mother had raced from her side and Chris was left to finish the trail alone.

The crying became louder, and raised voices were added to the noise.

The P.L. ran through the gate of the park. Then she stopped dead. The two women were having a tug of war with the baby boy, who was now yelling lustily, while the stalker tried vainly to intercede.

"Chris—Chris!" cried Bunny in desperation, and, without any very clear idea of what she was going to do, Chris ran swiftly towards the group.

CHAPTER 12

THE KING'S FLIGHT

IN the very moment at which the P.L. started forward, she heard quick, heavy footsteps behind her and a man's form swung past her.

The newcomer reached the scene of the commotion ahead of Chris, and, taking in the situation at a glance, grasped the shoulder of the woman in blue.

"Mrs. Potts," he said firmly but not unkindly. "What does this mean?"

At once the woman let go her hold on the child and raised a pair of anguished eyes to his.

"Mr. Scott!" she said. Her lips trembled, and a torrent of tears poured down her cheeks. For a few moments the sound of her uncontrollable sobbing kept the group silent. Then as Chris reached them, the newcomer—a man in his early forties, clad in a grey suit and clerical collar, whom Chris immediately recognized as the Rev. James Scott, minister of her own church—turned to the baby's mother.

"Can you trust me to handle this alone?" he asked her quietly. "This lady is a member of my church. She lost her own baby a few months ago. I can guess what has just happened, but she isn't quite responsible, you understand?"

The mother's face softened for a moment; then it hardened again, and she said sharply, "But she shouldn't be let loose to do this kind of thing! If she isn't locked up she'll try it again. It's not right to let her go."

The minister nodded, his grown eyes serious.

"It wouldn't be," he agreed, "if no one were willing to be responsible for her. But I can promise you there'll be no recurrence. I've a plan to direct that hunger of hers into a channel that will be helpful to other people as well as saving her reason, I believe."

He turned to Chris, who was standing silently beside him.

"This young woman will vouch for my integrity of character—won't you, Chris?" he said, with sudden laughter lines playing at the corners of his eyes. "And here is my card, with my name, address, and telephone number, if you should want to contact me at any time."

With her precious baby boy safely in her arms, the young mother smiled for the first time.

"All right, I'll leave it to you, Mr—er—Scott." She verified the name with a quick peep at his visiting card. "Now I'd better hurry back and collect my pram or I'll find that gone too!"

Awkwardly she touched the arm of the young woman in blue, whose sobs had now nearly died away. Then she turned on her heel and hurried off.

Mr. Scott put his arm around Mrs. Potts.

"I think a cup of coffee would do you the world of good, my dear," he said gently. "Come with me to The Manse and my wife will brew some. Then we'll have a little chat."

He turned to Chris. "I'd like a word with you, too, one evening next week, if you can spare the time. Is Thursday any good, or have you too much homework?"

Chris thought rapidly. It was History prep. that evening, and she always got through it fairly quickly.

"I can easily manage that," she told him.

"All right. I'll see you at The Manse as soon after seven o'clock as you can manage," he said cheerily. "I've been wanting a chat with you for several weeks now. Ever since you began turning up regularly to the Sunday services with a shining face, in fact!" he added, the laughter lines crinkling the corner of his eyes again; and Chris flushed with pleasure as she felt the warmth that lay behind the lightly spoken words.

As she made her way to The Manse five nights

later, Chris was divided between curiosity and a slight feeling of nervousness. But the nervousness soon dissolved under the friendly welcome she received.

"And how is the Poppy Patrol faring?" Mr. Scott asked genially, as she dropped into a chair in his study.

She gazed at him in astonishment, not having realized he even knew she was a Guide.

His brown eyes twinkled, but he offered no explanation of his knowledge. Instead, he waited for her reply—and within a few moments the Poppy P.L. was pouring out a lively account of their latest exploits.

"What are you going to do to raise funds for your dog, Kim, during the winter?" he asked with interest, when the account came to an end.

"Oh, we're each going to do something different," she told him, warming to her subject again. "We discussed it at Guides this week. We've each got 2*s*. to trade with. I'm going to make peppermint creams for a start. Then, when I've raised enough capital, I'm going to make handy little housewife's dollies to sell."

His eyes opened wide.

"I didn't know housewives played with dolls," he said in bewilderment. "I must ask Mrs. Scott about this!"

Chris chuckled.

"They're not ordinary dolls," she explained. "They're made up of kitchen utensils. You put a dish-mop and a wooden spoon back to back. Then you paint a face on the spoon, pad the handles with a sponge and pot-scourer, and dress the 'doll' in a duster. They're great fun and very useful."

"So I should imagine," agreed the minister. "And what are the rest of your Patrol doing?"

Chris considered for a moment.

"Bunny—that's the girl who was with me on Saturday morning—collects coloured postcards of birds and flowers, and she's going to mount them on white card and make calendars. Julie is planning to produce fancy boxes of homemade bath salts, and her sister is going to make face-cloths from a length of towelling. My Second, Sandra, who's keen on gardening, says she's going to sell little, potted plants. She'll make the pots from old gramophone records softened in hot water and moulded into shape. And Elizabeth is going to knit babies' bootees and mittens. As Christmas is ahead we thought our best plan would be to make things that would do for little Christmas presents."

Mr. Scott nodded. "You're certainly an enterprising Patrol, and I'm glad you've shared your interests with me, Chris. Now I'll tell you what I specially wanted to see you about."

She looked at him enquiringly, and he went on: "I may be wrong, of course, but I have the impression that something happened to you—spiritually—a few weeks ago. Until that time, I used to look down from my pulpit on a rather bored-looking Chris! Now I see a bright and happy face on Sundays, and I'd like you to share with me, if you will, the experience that lies behind that transformation—presuming I'm right in my conjecture, I mean."

Chris nodded shyly.

"I asked Jesus to come into my heart," she said simply, and she told him of her chat with Andrea and what had followed.

"Good for you, Chris," said the minister quietly. "So now the Lord Jesus Christ is in control of your life, with no rooms or even cupboards locked against Him, eh?"

She looked at him uncertainly.

"I don't quite understand what you mean about rooms and cupboards," she ventured.

He smiled. "That's just my way of saying that the really dedicated Christian lets Him into every part of her life, gives Him the key of every door. Some people, you know, keep Him out of the Friendship room of their lives. They say they've the right to choose any friends they like, regardless of whether they'll be a help or hindrance to their spiritual life. Others keep Him out of the Money room of their lives—arguing that their money is their own to do what they like with, and forgetting that it is really *His* money and they are only stewards of it. Do you follow me?"

"I think so," Chris said hesitantly.

"Others keep Him out of the Leisure room of their lives, saying that they're free to spend their leisure time just as they like," Mr. Scott went on. "But the Christian who has given Christ *all* the keys, let's Him guide her in all things. And she is the one who has learned the secret of a happy life! Think about that on your way home, Chris. It's tremendously important. And now, would you like me to tell you about Mrs. Potts?"

Chris nodded eagerly. She had been greatly wondering how the minister was going to help this unhappy soul. The answer, when he gave it, seemed to her to be perfect! A crèche was to be organized in the church hall during morning service each Sunday, for the benefit of mothers with young children—a team of ladies from the church, under the direction of Mrs. Scott herself, caring for the babies and toddlers while their parents worshipped without distraction. And Mrs. Potts was to be one of that team.

"Oh, could *I* help too, Mr. Scott?" Chris asked eagerly. "I've got my Child Nurse badge."

He hesitated.

"I'd rather you came to the service," he admitted. "But I was going to ask you if you could come down to The King's Flight on Sunday afternoons. You know about it, of course?"

Chris shook her head. "Is it Sunday school?"

"Yes and no," he told her. "There are no classes. The youngsters are divided into groups, each group being the crew and passengers of a civil aircraft, such as the *Constellation*, *Viking*, *Boeing*, and so on. A crew consists of the pilot, second pilot, navigator, and steward, and the new boys and girls who are brought along by the crew become the passengers. The chairs in the hall are arranged in the formation of an aircraft's wing. And the idea behind the name The King's Flight is that they are all in the service of the King of kings, and, like the crews of real planes, always on their toes ready for action."

Chris's eyes were sparkling. This sounded far more interesting than ordinary Sunday school, she decided.

"Instead of getting points for different things," the minister went on, "they have 'miles' credited to them. For example, 25 miles for bringing their Bibles, 25 for bringing themselves, 25 for wearing their badge—a silver aircraft against a sky-blue background—50 miles for doing their 'homework' and so on. The homework may be a Bible quiz or learning a short passage from the Bible. If they bring along a passenger to The King's Flight they gain still more miles for their aircraft. Boys or girls who turn up of their own accord become members of the ground staff instead of passengers."

"And what do they do with the miles?" Chris wanted to know.

The minister smiled. "They total them at the end of a month and then plot a course on a map, with little flags bearing the name of the different aircraft. Their destination for December might be Bethlehem, and they'll work out from their mileage which craft gets nearest. This month I believe they're following the Apostle Paul on one of his missionary journeys! They love the friendly rivalry. But there's good, constructive Bible teaching introduced, too, in an interesting manner; and if you want to grow into a really mature Christian, Chris, I'd strongly urge you to join them."

Chris beamed up into his face.

"I don't need urging," she said happily. "I'm going to become one of the ground staff this very Sunday!"

CHAPTER 13

HAPPY BIRTHDAY, CHRIS!

CHRIS uncrumpled the ear on which she had been lying crookedly, gave a big yawn, and stretched herself luxuriously in bed. Five to seven. She had five more minutes in which to lie and think about getting up.

Then a sudden thought struck her, and she shot out of bed like a pebble propelled from a catapult. She had just remembered something. Today was her fourteenth birthday!

Hurrying into the bathroom she had a mere apology for a wash, gave her teeth a lightning brush, and then ran back to the bedroom to scramble into her clothes. Five minutes later she was downstairs, rosy-cheeked and panting, an expectant gleam in her eyes.

"Happy birth lay, darling!" her mother greeted her, hastily putting the last of the birthday parcels on her daughter's plate. "You've raced both Daddy and Colin this morning. What a pity you haven't a birthday every day!"

They laughed companionably together, and Chris went through her pile of parcels, carefully feeling them all in turn without removing the wrappings. It would be cheating to open them before breakfast.

By the time the family had finished their cereal and boiled eggs, the postman had arrived, and more parcels—and a little stack of birthday cards—were added to the pile.

On a chair by itself stood a large, heavy package, carefully swathed in cardboard and brown paper. Chris had been eyeing it longingly throughout breakfast, and the very moment they finished eating she made a rush for it. Pulling off the wrappings she disclosed a magnificent crimson-and-white record player!

"Oh, *thank* you, Daddy and Mummy!" Her face was one huge beam. Several of the older girls at school had record players and were able to converse during break about the latest Pop discs and singers in a sophisticated manner. Now she would be one of them, suddenly grown-up and knowledgeable.

A record token from Colin came spinning through the air and settled neatly on her plate. She flashed him a grateful smile as she saw the value stamped on it. She would be able to exchange it for *two* records. What dears her family were!

Beautiful, polished, wooden book-ends from

Andrea Whitfield, carved in the shape of the Guide trefoil, nestled in tissue paper in her next parcel. Chris stared at them in astonishment. How had Miss Whitfield known it was her birthday? Then she opened a little badge-cleaning outfit in a blue plastic case—a present from the faithful Bunny—and she realized who had given away the secret!

A pocket sewing-kit in a leather case stamped with the Guide badge was her next discovery, followed by a yellow-and-blue propelling pencil with the same familiar badge plus the words *Girl Guides Association* stamped on it in gold. The Poppies had all got wind of their Leader's birthday and had clubbed together.

There were several letters from relations, each containing money gifts; there was a chocolate-filled cash box, complete with lock and key, from her school chum, and birthday cards from the immediate family and some of the girls at school.

Mrs. Temple looked anxiously at the clock.

"Hadn't you better leave them all now?" she suggested gently. "I'll put them up in your Den for you and you can enjoy them again when you come home this evening."

Chris reluctantly put them down. Then she picked up Bunny's badge-cleaning outfit and gave her Guide and King's Flight badges a quick polish before restoring them to the lapel of her blazer. She had been presented with the blue-and-silver badge after four consecutive attendances at The King's Flight, and had incidentally distinguished herself—and added 100 miles to her aircraft's total—by introducing Bunny as a passenger on her fourth Sunday!

She glanced quickly at the clock, pocketed her record token, postal orders, and two treasury notes, and hurried off to get her hat and coat. Five minutes later the door slammed behind her.

Mrs. Temple smiled indulgently. She could just remember what it felt like to be exactly fourteen years old.

She wondered idly, as she cleared the breakfast table, what her young daughter was going to do with all that money. She'd save some of it, no doubt. Chris was mostly very wise with money, and would put it into her birthday cashbox.

But Chris had other ideas. Completely forgetting Mr. Scott's little word about asking God for guidance in all things, she had rashly allocated every penny of it to her newly born craze for Pop records!

The day passed slowly, and Chris had considerable difficulty in concentrating on her lessons.

When she was finally released from school she

hurried to the big radio and record shop in the High Street. During break that morning she had compiled a list of Pop discs recommended by some fifth-formers, and now, armed with that list and conscious of the fact that she had gone up in their estimation, she was ready to do business.

The alert salesman in the shop was more than ready to assist her. He offered to play the discs over to her before packing them up, but Chris had no time for that. It was her Guide night. If she hurried through her tea, she decided, she would be able to run them through in her Den.

Colin had not got in from school when she reached home, and her mother was at a women's meeting at church. Chris accordingly had a rushed tea and then took her precious records up to her Den, where Mrs. Temple had carefully laid out all her presents.

Her heart beat quickly as she put the first disc into position. A few moments later her foot was tapping rhythmically to the sound. This was fun! Her face fell, after a little, though. The beat was good, but that was about all. . . .

By the time she had played through three of them she was feeling distinctly disillusioned. Was this what the fifth-formers raved about? Surely one would get tired of them very soon!

She pulled the shop receipt out of her pocket and looked ruefully at the total. Her sudden impulse had cost her dear.

A tap at the door caused her to start guiltily. Mrs. Temple peeped in.

"Enjoying the new record player, dear?" she asked with unconscious irony. "That's good! You must let me hear your new records some time. I'll go and get tea now."

Colin's red head appeared in the doorway immediately afterwards.

"You haven't exchanged your record token yet, have you?" he enquired. "I've brought you a list of recordings. Some of your specials are here: Beethoven's *Fifth*, some Chopin *Nocturnes*, your favourite *Piano Concerto in A Minor* by Grieg, and——"

He broke off and looked at her intently.

"What's the matter, old girl?" he asked with concern.

"Oh, Colin—I've spent all my birthday money *and* your token and I've bought some discs I don't like a bit."

Colin looked bewildered. "But why did you buy them if you didn't like them?"

"I couldn't wait to hear them first, because of Guides tonight. I just went on the recommendation of some of the older girls at school. I wish I'd waited for your lists. The shop'll never give me my money back," she added in despair.

He picked up the discs in turn and read the labels. Then he whistled softly.

"My! You have gone to town on Pop," he said. "I shouldn't have thought it was your cup of tea at all. You'll tire of it in no time!"

Chris's lips quivered, and Colin patted her shoulder awkwardly. "It's no use crying over spilt milk, Sis. As you say, they won't change them at the shop now that you've played them, but I've got 10*s*. in stamps on my National Savings card. I'll cash them and you can have the money to give you a fresh start. Cheer up, now! We all have to learn from experience."

As he clumped downstairs in his heavy, school shoes, the tears, which Chris had tried so hard to restrain, began to flow—partly because of Colin's generosity and partly because Chris had at last remembered her talk with Mr. Scott and realized that she had been a bad steward.

"That must have been what he meant by locking a cupboard!" she suddenly exclaimed aloud.

She had thought her Money room was open to the Lord Jesus. Mummy always said she was good with money. But she had reserved the right to spend her birthday money without first asking for guidance, and that was the locked cupboard in the room!

"The Christian who has given Christ *all* the keys, let's Him guide her in all things." Chris heard the words again so clearly that it almost seemed as if Mr. Scott was in the room. She pulled out her hanky and dried her eyes. But it was no good. She felt a sense of utter failure and the tears continued to flow.

CHAPTER 14

A CHAPTER OF 'ACCIDENTS'

HALF an hour later Chris set off for Guides, humming a little tune below her breath.

Gone were the tears. She had suddenly remembered that Andrea had told her only the other evening that, when a Christian was really sorry for grieving the Lord Jesus, if she told Him so from a contrite heart He would fully forgive her. And that was exactly what Chris had done!

She arrived in her Patrol corner just in time to thank the Poppies gratefully for their birthday gifts, before a series of short blasts on Captain's whistle brought the Guides running to her from all corners of the Guide Hut. In her hand she held a copy of *The Guide* magazine.

"Hands up those who take *The Guide* each week," she said, and nearly a dozen hands were raised.

She smiled her approval and pointed to a recent issue of it which lay on the table. "Those of you who have read this copy will know that there's a splendid article in it on doll-making, entitled *Dolls with Character*."

The Guides who had raised their hands nodded vigorously, and she continued: "For the benefit of the rest of you I'll explain that it gives instructions for making dolls from old stockings and worn-out undies (or, in fact, any wool or silk material near flesh colour), with lots of diagrams showing how to dress them in the costumes of other countries and how to give them suitable features and hair-styles according to their different nationalities. Well, Lieutenant suggested, at the Court of Honour last week, that we might all spend a part of our Company evenings between now and Christmas in making lots of these dolls for the Children's Home. And Clare thought we should also go through our treasures at home and see what we could spare in the way of discarded books and outgrown toys, in good condition, to add to our gifts."

There was a general buzz of approval.

"It will mean getting all our friends and relations to turn out their scrap bags to help with the material for the dolls, so we must get down to that bit of the job right away," Captain went on. "The other gifts can come later. Rose suggested that we should give the children a Christmas party, too! As you know, the Fuchsias have been doing very useful Patrol Service at the Home recently, and they feel that a special Christmas treat would highly delight the children. How does the idea appeal to the rest of you?"

There was a chorus of "Oh, yes!" and "Do let's!" from the others.

"It's going to take a lot of organizing, but I certainly think it would be worthwhile," the Guider agreed. "Does anyone want to add to those suggestions for Christmas, while we're on the subject?"

Sudden inspiration came to Chris.

"If we're going to make dolls from other countries," she said, "couldn't we end with a carol item and sing carols from other countries, too? Daddy's got a book of them that I expect he'd lend us."

Captain turned to Lieutenant with a smile. "You're the musical one. Do you think you could teach us all to sing some new carols? If so, I think Chris's idea is excellent."

Lieutenant chuckled. "I'm willing—provided you'll have the piano tuned first. It's shockingly flat, at the moment!"

"We'll soon have that little matter put right," Captain promised her with a smile. "Then there will be the refreshments to think about. I'm sure Matron would arrange the basic food and drink, but it would be rather nice if we could provide some exciting extras for the children. Grace could make them some of her special mince-pies and——" She broke off. "Where *is* Grace, by the way? She seems to be missing."

"She hasn't turned up tonight," the Fuchsia P.L. reported. "I don't know why."

Captain nodded briefly and continued: "There's the little matter of decorating the hall, too. Probably the Poppies will be able to gather holly from Sir Roderick's grounds as they're good friends of his, and I believe the Home has a Christmas tree which they bring out each year."

Bunny hopped up and down with excitement.

"We c-could decorate the tree with coloured f-felt cut into different shapes and stuck on cardboard," she said. "You stick sequins on them to m-make them glisten, and they hang by a loop of t-tinsel. We learned how to do them at B-brownies."

"Splendid!" commented Captain, with a twinkle in her eye. "We'll put you in charge of the Decorations Patrol."

Bunny's green eyes opened wide with distress.

"Oh, no, I c-couldn't," she exclaimed anxiously, and Chris quickly whispered that Captain was only teasing her.

"Well, off you go now to your Corners for Patrol subscriptions," the Guider instructed them, and there was a general scuffle of feet as the Guides ran off.

Suddenly the door opened, and the missing Fuchsia stumbled in.

"I—I——" she faltered, and then fell in a crumpled heap on the ground. The Guides instinctively turned to where Captain stood at a distance talking to Lieutenant, their backs to the scene, apparently unconscious of what was happening.

"She's fainted!" exclaimed Penelope. "Quick! Lay her out straight, with her feet raised on this chair." She turned to her Second. "Get a glass of water for when she comes round, and the rest of you stand back and give her air."

She was loosening Grace's tie and opening the neck of her blouse, as she spoke.

"She's awfully pale," commented Sandra. "I wonder what made her faint?"

She looked more closely at the recumbent figure, and then said suspiciously, "She's got *chalk* all over her face. I believe it's a hoax!"

Grace grinned and sat up, and the indignant Guides looked towards the Guiders again. They were quietly watching the scene, with little smiles on their faces.

"Don't you remember my saying last week that, having got the necessary theory of first aid, you needed practice so that you'd learn to keep your head in an emergency and not panic?" Captain asked them. "Well, we arranged a little emergency for you this evening! When you've collected your Patrol subscriptions, Leaders, I want each Patrol to demonstrate an accident in turn, and show how you would tackle the situation. The Pansies can do a street accident, the Fuchsias a rescue from drowning, and the Poppies a rescue from fire."

The Guides looked at each other gleefully. This was going to be fun, and it would be particularly useful for those of them who were working towards their First Class badge.

"We'll have Bunny for our casualty, because she's smallest," announced Chris, as soon as she had collected the Poppies' subscriptions. "Sandra, you'd better be the one to drag her to safety, as you're our heftiest member. Elizabeth, you can be the one to raise the alarm in the first place. We must remember to treat Bunny for shock afterwards, or we'll lose points."

In the Fuchsia and Pansy corners, equally enthusiastic planning was taking place.

At last, Captain blew a long blast on her whistle for silence; then she instructed the Pansies to begin their demonstration while the remainder of the Company sat round in a circle.

The Pansies had thought it out well, and the whole scene was presented efficiently—the car swinging round the corner and the old lady knocked down, the phone box call for the ambulance, the directing of traffic away from the scene of the accident, the keeping back of the spectators, and the treatment for shock.

"They've thought of everything," Chris whispered to Sandra. "Ours will have to be very good to compete with that!"

The Fuchsias followed. They pretended to do balancing feats on a breakwater, and inevitably one fell into the sea. Another dived to the rescue and brought her out. Then came the necessary artificial respiration and the treatment for shock.

"That was good, too," Chris acknowledged to herself.

Then it was the Poppies' turn.

"Hurry up and rescue me, once we start, in case I burn to a c-cinder," said Bunny with a giggle.

"You're more likely to have your head bumped off as I pull you along the floor," Sandra told her cheerfully. "Come on—we're starting. Get into your house."

Sandra linked her arm through Elizabeth's and the pair strolled nonchalantly across the hut. Suddenly Elizabeth gave a shout of "Fire!" and pointed dramatically to the house made of chairs. Then she dashed off to the nearest call-box and dialled 999, leaving Sandra to rescue Bunny, who was now screaming realistically.

Outside the house, Sandra pulled off her scarf and, after holding it under an imaginary water tap in the kitchen, covered her nose and mouth with it. Then she soaked her triangular Guide tie under the same tap and covered her hair.

"Good girl!" Captain commented quietly to Lieutenant.

Next she crept into the building on hands and knees to avoid getting suffocated by the smoke. Reaching Bunny with difficulty, she tied her wrists together with Bunny's own tie, put them over her head and slowly crawled out, dragging Bunny along on her back. Then Chris appeared on the scene and treated her for shock.

Bunny rose to her feet, scarlet in the face with excitement and exertion, as the demonstration ended, and they all looked enquiringly at the two Guiders.

"You did well—all three Patrols," Captain told them warmly. "Congratulations! There was little to choose between you, but I think perhaps the Poppies take first place because theirs was particularly tricky. I was afraid poor Bunny was going to get her head bumped on the floor as Sandra dragged her out of her burning house, but you managed splendidly, Sandra."

On the way home from the meeting, Bunny was full of it all.

"I l-like Surprise Evenings," she said rapturously. "I hope we have another one soon! I like The King's Flight, too," she added unexpectedly. "I'm g-glad you took me along, Chris."

The P.L. beamed. "I'm glad you like it, Bunny. I thought somehow you would."

"Chris——" Bunny looked at her diffidently as they reached the parting of the ways. "When the F-flight Officer asked how many of us would open our hearts to Jesus, you didn't p-put up your hand."

Chris smiled. "I didn't need to, Bunny. I'd already asked Him to come in some weeks ago. But you didn't raise yours either!"

The little Poppy flushed.

"I was afraid, C-Chris," she said.

Chris looked at her in astonishment. "But there's nothing to be afraid of, you silly one! I've been heaps happier since I did it." And she told her of her chat with Andrea, and of Mr. Scott's talk about handing over all the keys.

"Th-that's what I'm afraid of," returned Bunny, her green eyes looking pathetic.

"But surely you can trust the One who gave His life for you," Chris pointed out logically. "If He loves you like that, then He's the best One to be in control of your life! Mr. Scott said that, if the world really saw Christ living in people, they'd be attracted to Christianity instead of being sceptical about it all."

But Bunny turned away, her shoulders drooping. She was counting the cost of discipleship and the price was too high.

As Chris continued her journey alone, she felt nearly as unhappy as Bunny. The smallest Poppy was in spiritual need and she felt powerless to help her.

She thought of the Bible reading one of the Technicians had given the previous Sunday, from the first chapter of John's Gospel. Andrew had brought his brother to the Lord Jesus, and Philip had brought Nathanael; and they had both become His disciples. Where had she failed with Bunny?

Perhaps it was different when He was on earth, she thought despondently. Then her face brightened as the answer to her problem struck her. She couldn't bring Bunny physically to Jesus, *but she could bring her to Him in prayer*—and He would do the rest!

She gave a happy, little skip as she inserted her key in her front-door lock.

CHAPTER 15

A DIFFICULT CHOICE

CHRIS stacked the silver and coppers into neat little piles, a happy smile on her face. The Poppies had worked tirelessly during the past weeks, each trading with her 2*s*. Now, with Christmas near, Chris had called in the proceeds and had found to her delight that the original 12*s*. had brought in a total of £8 3*s*. 9*d*. for their Kim fund.

She slipped the money into a strong, bank envelope, loaned by her father, and wrote Sir Roderick's name on it. Then she turned her attention to another absorbing matter—the choosing of gifts for the Children's Home Christmas party.

Lightly she ran her fingers over the tops of the books on the bookshelves which lined her Den. She had been collecting books for years. Her childhood favourites still rubbed shoulders with her more mature taste in reading, so the shelves were well filled. One by one she put the chosen volumes on the floor, all of them suitable for little folk.

"No—too shabby," she commented, returning three of them to the shelves. Hadn't Captain emphasized the need for gifts in good condition?

At last she had selected a dozen titles, all favourites of hers and in any other circumstances not easy to part with. But this was something special. She felt it was almost like giving them to the Lord Jesus Himself, for the Bible reading at The King's Flight last week had contained those lovely words 'Inasmuch as ye have done it unto one of the least of these my brethren, ye have done it unto me'.

Reaching for her school bag, she fitted the twelve books neatly inside and strapped them up tightly, ready to take down to Guides.

Two streets away, Bunny was busy at the same occupation. But she was not finding it nearly as easy or satisfying as Chris.

On the floor in front of where she sat cross-legged on the carpet, was a monkey with an ear hanging loose and an eye missing, a one-armed doll, a rabbit she had never much cared for, and a story book with some of the pictures torn out. And, try as she would, she could think of nothing to add to the little collection.

There was her beautiful golden-haired teddy bear, Rufus, who always sat on her bed, but she couldn't spare *him*, of course. There were some jolly table games too, but they were almost new. Nobody could expect her to part with those. As for her toy gramophone with records, Mummy would be awfully cross if she gave that away, even if she wanted to, for it had cost a lot of money.

She looked at the crocks on the floor. There would fortunately be no wrench in parting with any of them; in fact it was high time they were thrown out to make room for newcomers. But something inside her wouldn't let her be quite happy about them. They were, she had to admit, a very maimed collection.

Then Sunday afternoon's Bible reading flashed into Bunny's mind, followed by some words from the closing hymn:

I gave My life for thee.
What hast Thou given to Me?

And her cheeks flushed hotly.

For a few moments the battle raged; then, stiffening her lip, Bunny pushed the motley collection into the corner of the room and reached for Rufus.

CHAPTER 16

THE CHRISTMAS PARTY

CHRIS fanned her hot cheeks and took a long, cool sip of lemonade. Then she smiled gaily across the decorated hall at Captain.

The party was certainly proving a success! Forty excited children, wearing the coloured paper hats they had found inside their Christmas crackers, had played all their favourite musical games to Lieutenant's accompaniment on the piano. They had received a surprise visit from Father Christmas, who presented them with gifts from the Christmas tree, and they had been given the attractively dressed dolls from other countries. Afterwards they had eaten their fill of Grace's mincepies, plus an enormous Christmas cake made by Captain's mother, while listening to Christmas music played on Chris's record player. And now the grand finale was to be presented to them!

It had been unanimously decided, some weeks ago, to abandon the carols from other countries in favour of the Christmas Story read from the Bible by Captain, with well-known Christmas hymns and carols sung at intervals by the Company. Now at a signal from Captain, the Guides grouped themselves informally around her as she sat with the closed Book on her knee. The chattering children grew quieter, their watchful eyes following every movement.

Bunny glanced towards the tiny tots among them as she sped across the hall to take up her position, and what she saw brought a sudden rush of happiness to her heart. In their midst sat Rufus, and they were touching him with reverent fingers, their eyes alight with wonder and delight.

From somewhere behind the grouped Guides came the strains of music, played softly by Lieutenant as a prelude. Then Captain opened the Bible and began to read, with fifty pairs of eyes focused solemnly upon her. Most of the audience were old enough to follow the story from Isaiah and Luke, but even the tinies felt the sense of awe and worship in the atmosphere.

Chris looked at the wrapt faces in front of her, watching their changing expressions. Then, as Captain read ". . . And suddenly there was with the angel a multitude of the heavenly host, praising God," the music of *Hark, the herald angels sing* sounded quietly, and the Guides broke into the well-loved carol, joined by the intent audience.

The reading continued throughout the lovely

story, interspersed with the appropriate carols, and as Captain closed the Book the Guides quietly stood for their final hymn: *Thou didst leave Thy throne and Thy kingly crown, when Thou camest to earth for me. . . .*

It was as they reached the refrain at the end of the first verse that Chris suddenly caught sight of Bunny. The youngest Poppy had her very soul in her eyes as she sang:

Oh, come to my heart, Lord Jesus,
There is room in my heart for Thee,

and Chris knew that her prayer was answered. Andrew had brought Simon to Jesus, Philip had brought Nathanael, and Chris had brought Bunny. And they had *all* become disciples!

"I meant what I s-sang," Bunny told her eagerly, when the party was over. "I opened my heart to Him tonight, and I'm g-going to tell Miss Whitfield when she comes carol-singing with us on Monday night. Will she bring Judy with her, so that the people will s-see what we're collecting for?"

Chris nodded happily. "She promised she would; and she can sing alto, so the carols ought to sound good." She pulled on her coat and helped Bunny into hers. "Do you realize that we've known her for exactly six months now? What a lot of exciting things have happened in that time!"

Bunny beamed at her.

"I guess there's even more exciting th-things ahead," she said with satisfaction.

THE END